The most beautiful garden

by
Nikita Rimal Sharma

illustrations by
Alexa Laharty

YELLOW ARROW
PUBLISHING
Baltimore, Maryland, USA

Library of Congress Control Number: 2022934270
ISBN (paperback): 979-8-9850704-0-8

Cover and interior art by Alexa Laharty (Instagram @alexaelisabeth).
Interior design by Isabelle Anderson.
For more information, see yellowarrowpublishing.com.

Dedicated to my parents, Papa and Taa

I am who I am because of you (Ma j chu, timi haru le garda chu).

We may never have had the best of things but that is never what I needed anyway.

Taa,
If not for you, I would never know how to seek joy in little things, dance like no one is watching and laugh without limits. The most important thing I learned by being in your shadow as a child is to give love unconditionally and without boundaries. Whether it was our local tailor, vegetable seller, or your own children, I saw you treat everyone equally, respectfully, never hesitating to give a hug, a compliment, an ear to listen to, or a shoulder to cry on. When giving, the boundaries of social status and caste to you never exist. I will carry that way of loving as long as I live, for there is no greater thing than love.

Papa,
If not for you, I would have never learned how to accept and embrace myself. You always encouraged me to follow my heart and do more of the things that bring me joy and reflect my strengths. One of my favorite childhood memories is of our weekly trip to buy books and magazines; words have been my true love since. With the resilience, patience, and courage with which you manage your health, you have given me wisdom so deep. I have come to find that true growth and success are about accepting yourself where you are and getting up, fall after fall. If I have half the strength you have, I know I will be fine no matter the challenges in life.

You both have given me a voice of strength, maybe not the loudest, but very mighty, fueled by compassion and authenticity. You gave me everything I need and with these tools, I will continue to grow in ways that are meaningful to me. I am who I am because of you. Ma je chu timi harule garda chu.

Contents

Acknowledgments

I don't think this book would have been possible had I not joined the first ever "Poetry is Life" class by Ann Quinn. I am forever grateful for that. Gratitude on the same level also goes to Yellow Arrow Publishing for providing a platform and to my "Poetry is Life" classmates for providing me with inspiration.

All my lovely friends from childhood until adulthood, my family, cousins, coworkers, and everyone else (you know who you are), who have shown me understanding and space as I navigate my life and grow. I am always thankful for you all.

"The most beautiful garden" was published in *Poetry is Life: Writing with Yellow Arrow* by Yellow Arrow Publishing (2022).

THE MOST BEAUTIFUL GARDEN

(not) just a matchstick

An oak log on a chilly day:
I wanted to be
element of warmth, spreader of light
center of all gatherings.

A mere matchstick
I thought myself to be,
feeble in structure.
Needing several strikes for a single second of flame.

Until I realized
unseen in its glory, I may be
lighter of other light sources.
I still can be.

The places that made me

Dirt and grime, loud horns, narrow alley and big dreams
Kathmandu is the root to my being:
fertilized by my mother's unconditional love
my father's quiet ways
my brother's companionship;
some seeds left to die with the poisonous toxicity of societal pressure.

Wichita was the blank canvas for the rest of my life:
under the bright blue sky, amidst the open fields
wrapped in my lover's supportive arm,
I started to carve a new chapter
for the rest of my life.

Baltimore is the city that helped me fly:
fabricated with wings of struggles and growth,
I shed my skin of the insecurity and fear I held,
and started to find
people, places, ideas, and actions that make my life divine.

House of anxiety

My mind has built
a clear glass house.
From where I stand, I can see
EVERYTHING
go from bad to worse;
fall apart;
watch nightmares come true.

I continue to live inside it
falsely protected.
Willingly and unwillingly
I stay in,
not yet ready to shatter the walls,
and find if they are all in fact true.

Growth

The sediment of our childhood
is the soil on which we grow.
Optimally fertilized and nourished in some parts,
rocky and dehydrated in others.

It is up to us
to remain a sapling
or
give ourselves the permission
to dig deeper,
clear the debris,
allow the flow of love and warmth, to grow into a tree that bears fruit.

Fire and water (city life vs. nature)

Bright lights from skyscrapers
light a fire in my heart
to turn every dream into reality.

Surrounded by nature,
with stars as my blanket,
birds chirping as my music,
I become one with the mountain,
accepting and embracing where I am.

One lifts, the other grounds.
One inspires, the other calms.
Like elements of fire and flowing water,
the places I visit
help me be found.

Music of your life

Dearest,
when in doubt
put your hand on your heart
breathe
deeper.

Swim to the deepest layer
listen to the voice
slowly
patiently
bravely

let those words write
the song of your life.
The rhythm may not be perfect,
but it will be yours.

Raindrops on my window

Things you notice when you slow down:

a droplet of rain runs through my windowpane and joins another droplet.

They flow together as if they were never separate.

Maybe this is how we can make the world a better place?

Try to love people when it's hard for you to love:
love them when they don't talk your talk or walk your walk.
Let the wings of your heart fly to places it doesn't want to go.

Give people the love you usually give after they die:
forgiveness for everything they aren't,
gratitude for everything they are.

Love is most beautiful when it's without conditions.

Sibling love

Babu!

Then,
you were my partner in many of my firsts—
my first bicycle ride,
my first wall climb.

Now,
as we live our stories
of not just the firsts
but numerous moments of
heartaches, wins, lessons, and love,
you are still my partner
making my loads lighter and my smiles brighter.

The most beautiful garden

My Taa dresses up every day,
in the brightest shades of yellow and red.
"You are dressed like a garden," I say.

And a garden she is,
perhaps a bed of lotus,
with muddy foundations of patriarchy.

Or maybe she has morphed into
a fragrant bush of roses—
enamored by beauty,
guarded by thorns.

English is my second language

My tongue rolls thicker,
invites second glances when I say water.

In a foreign land,
language that is secondary
is considered primary
in the measurement of my talents and abilities.

Space

The space I take up with my voice
is not posters with black bold markers,
all caps,
firm and direct!

It is a canvas painting
of pastels and bright hues,
written with intention.

The space I take up with my voice
may not grab the same amount of attention or fury,

but I hope:
it makes you lie
on a bed of green grass
stare at the blue sky
and think of

kindness and healing,
for you and others.

Gunshots

62 in 2021 alone, from an Instagram post I just saw—
So many more I don't know of.

Emotions have started to turn numb
as . . .

lives continue to become statistics
certificates of death on paper
a mumble of thought or prayer
promises of justice through financial support.

What is justice when they are not lives anymore
living, breathing, growing,
perhaps making mistakes
but equally deserving of second chances
like other privileged, rich counterparts?

Unresolved trauma

Like crumbled letters from unrequited love,
I have in my heart
the remains of my childhood:
tales of the nets cast by patriarchy and
the dark shadow of privilege.

For so long,
I have left them
unread, unresolved, unshared,
adding clutter to my adult psyche.

Those stories
I reluctantly read in my mind now
to free myself,
from the ink of those letters
that have seeped into my bones
and name themselves: perfectionism, defense mechanism, anxiety,
and depression.

The only way to heal now
is to read those letters.
Let the tears flow
cut the nets
wipe the shadow

I am on my way . . .
to being whole again,
free again.

My beautiful body

My heart aches and flutters,
carries people and places wrapped in love.

My limbs have carried me to places,
and my loved ones in warm embraces.

Every cell, every organ,
works without complaint,
to keep me going.

Here I am,
continuing to measure my worth and sense by standing on a
weighing machine.

Forever, love!

I have loved running for a long time. The strides of one foot over the other, while I catch my breath, is a simple movement, yet it gives me a taste of freedom and a focus for my meditation.

I love running so much, I wanted it to be my source of glory and pride. I wanted to run for more:
multiple medals of 5Ks and 10Ks, the car sticker with 13.1 miles, a social media post with an inspiring story of how I finally challenged my younger, unathletic self and became a onetime half marathoner (a slow one, but one, nonetheless).

But running didn't love me back that way. After my 11-mile milestone, I injured my knees. It hurt me too much to walk up and down the stairs or take long walks. It crushed my goal and it crushed me. But that isn't the moral of this story.

I went for a run after a month today, just a mile and a half. Now, I have things to ponder. Here it goes.

Dear running,
I thought your feelings for me had changed.
I was wrong,
you have always remained the same.

In your name,
I wanted to chase the glory.
But all I truly needed
was how you made me feel,
not how you made me look.

I know that now,
so we will meet again,
perhaps far and in-between.

I am learning to love you in a different light,
slowly, gently,
without strings attached,
just as deep.

(Random) moments of my making

I learned about heartbreak at age five.
Papa bought me a lovely red balloon and it burst within five minutes.

At 10, I thought I was a superhero and went to wrestle with my
brother but always lost, still always got all the love and none of the
blame from my parents.
I was and am a pampered child.
Oh and the lovely trips with Papa to bookstores on Saturdays. He
also got me a milky bar on my way back. We didn't talk a lot, we
have never needed that.

Winter breaks from school meant afternoons spent snacking on
oranges and roasted peanuts, soaking up the sun's warmth,
having endless conversations with my Taa, about anything and
everything.
She has always been my best pal.
And when school closed for the festivities of Dashain and Tihar,
and home was filled with the smell of sel roti and achar,
the cool autumn breeze carried that smell afar,
seemingly making everything alright.

Now in my 30s,
I spend my days meditating, writing, reading, accepting, letting go,
growing, and glowing.
Keeping up the promise to be happy, healthy, and kind (to myself
        and others),
never do I want to be in the shoes of that girl on a cold January
        morning in 2016,
when the cashier at the grocery store was my only social contact.
I crumbled into bed in tears right after that.
Mental illness is not made up, ever.

Every random moment small or big has led me to all that I am today.

To my Taa

Your worth
is not in the words and actions of people
who have never had the appetite for your grace and beauty.

It is
in the time you get up, fall after fall.
It is
in the tears you hold back
and the pain you hide,
in the name of all the love you have to give.

Do not let another person's futile attempt to shatter you be your
weakness.
Let it kindle your fire to give more to those who matter.

Matriarchy

Her words: sharp and bitter.
Her ego: inflated too big without any place for love.
She holds power without grace,
greed without compassion,
love with very specific conditions,
pride that is unearned and undeserved.

When I was a kid who could be molded into anything, her presence
molded my limitations.
Her words, "You can't do it, don't touch that, this is not yours,"
seeped into my being as an inner voice that makes it easier to come
up with reasons to believe I am incapable of doing what I want to,
unworthy of receiving or giving love without conditions,
that I have had to spend the rest of my life working on.

I sometimes think what would have become of me if her presence
had never existed.
I realize I would have never learned who not to be.

To Theresa: my colleague and most of all, my dear friend on May 8, 2021

On the night you left the earth
the sky outside my window
sparkled with flames of fire
lighting up the dark.

Such were the lives you touched.
The fire in you
to see the best in others, for others
to advocate with persistence
lighted in others, too,
flames of empowerment and self-love.

I will miss you, my friend. I will try to carry you in my heart and
try to be half as strong as you for as long as I live.

Veranda on 332 Bagbazar Street

Adorned only with a simple jute rug to sit on,
I sat there on summer evenings, cool and breezy
on winter afternoons soaking up the sun,
as I let that world inside the walls
of a family too big
in numbers, space and ego
remain inside,
and let my mind travel to the taste of freedom,
my heart craft dreams and aspirations
not limited by patriarchy, privilege, and the dominance of inherited
wealth

Healing through poetry

Dear Anxiety,
With sweaty armpits at a dinner table, you are there,
awkwardly muttering, nodding
wanting to share, but only smiling.

With speedy heartbeats you are there,
behind the steering wheel
turn signal on
but barely moving.

With perfectionism,
you hide,
maybe this time no one will actually know what's going on inside.

With therapy,
you try,
one step at a time.

With poetry,
you start to heal.
Emotions are better managed when shared on paper.

Stone, the Pitbull Terrier

As the gray cloud of February cold
blanketed my depression in feelings of hopelessness,
his meaty body sat on my lap, barely fitting,
warm, tiger-striped, soft to the touch, strong,
smelling of lavender shampoo and musty rain.
Warming first my thighs
then my heart,
just like the feeling you get
when the sun peeks through the clouds after a rainy day.

You watered my wildflower roots

Lover,
You saw the twisted corners of my being
that are hard for me to like,
watered them with understanding, love, and space.

Your acceptance of all my parts
were the fertilizers and nourishment
the seeds of my adulthood needed.

Thank you, Prashant!

My flesh is not your pleasure

Sacred you call Goddess Durga in Dashain and Laxmi in Dipawali.
Emblems of love are the vagina that pushed you to life and breasts
that nourished your growth.
That greatness,
which lives in your faith, mother, sister, daughter,
is also embodied in the flesh, body, and soul,
of the woman you choose as the object of your desire.

Mental health of a South Asian woman

Society dictates her life:
"A good woman sacrifices, compromises, smiles always,
for the happiness of others is where a woman's purpose lies,"
they say.

Every sense of herself, she learns to define,
based on the needs of man-children and children.
Her individual voice now a background noise,
always there, never heard.

So she hides
behind the mask of vibrant red outfits and dangling bangles.
Sorrows gulped like tequila shots,
insides burning with the fire of unrequited dreams.

Truth comes out,
everything disguised is trauma expressed
with anxious thoughts and sleepless nights.

"A good woman sacrifices, compromises, smiles always,
for the happiness of others is where a woman's purpose lies,"
they said.
I wonder where they are now.

Dance floor of flavors

My tongue will perhaps never learn
to sway to the rhythm of salt and pepper.

It is used to dancing to the flavors
of masalas and chilies,
smacking, slurping,
just like my favorite Bollywood melody.

(With added special effects of sprinkled crushed red peppers.)

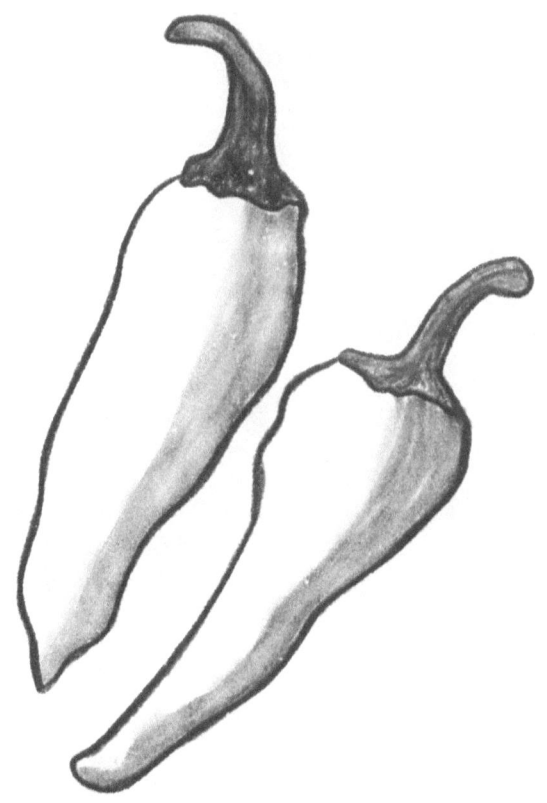

Nikita Rimal Sharma currently resides in Baltimore, Maryland with her husband and dog, Stone, and works at B'More Clubhouse, a community-based mental health nonprofit. She is originally from Kathmandu, Nepal. Nikita is a typical homebody who gets a lot of joy from slow running, short hikes, reading, and deep thoughts. She has always loved writing and started writing at the age of seven when she wrote a fairy tale titled "Star Girls." Nikita wishes she had saved a copy of it. Nikita's first published poem was in *Yellow Arrow Journal* **(Re)Formation** from fall 2020.

Find her on Instagram @nikita.playwithwords.

Thank you for supporting independent publishing.

Yellow Arrow Publishing is a nonprofit
supporting writers that identify as women. Visit
YellowArrowPublishing.com for information on our
publications, workshops, and writing opportunities.